UNRAVELING THE UNIVERSE

A BEGINNER'S GUIDE TO STRING THEORY

SIDDHARTH TALARI

CONTENTS

Author's Note

Ever since I was a young kid, I've been captivated by the mysteries of the universe. How did it all begin? What are the fundamental building blocks of reality? What rules and laws govern everything from the smallest particles to the largest galaxies? My curiosity only grew as I started devouring books and videos about cutting-edge physics ideas like quantum mechanics and Einstein's theories of relativity. The more I learned, the more I realized how much we still have left to understand about the cosmos and the strange quantum realm underlying it all. That's what first sparked my fascination with string theory - an ambitious framework that aims to construct a seamless, unified model encompassing all the particles, forces, and interactions we observe in the universe. String theory introduces brilliant and bizarre ideas like the existence of extra dimensions beyond the familiar three spatial ones we experience. It reimagines the fundamental "particles" making up matter as wildly vibrating, oscillating strings of energy.

At first, the mathematics and concepts of string theory seemed light years beyond my comprehension as a high school student. But the more I studied and immersed myself in the subject through books, lectures, discussions with teachers and the occasional expert I could get to respond to my endless questions, the more the core principles and philosophy started making sense. What emerged was a remarkably elegant, sweeping vision of reality - one where the fabric of space and time is just one piece of an intertwined, higher-dimensional cosmic tapestry. A vision where all the forces we observe today, from gravity to electromagnetism, arise from the resonant vibrations and harmonies of inconceivably small strings. And a vision suggesting our familiar universe may be just one piece of a grander multiverse composed of parallel realms. String theory opens up new perspectives on our origins as well. Many versions of the theory postulate that our universe emerged from an unimaginably hot, dense primordial string soup, rapidly inflating from a vanishingly small region and imprinting the seeds of cosmic structure we still observe today as temperature variations across the sky.

Despite its undeniable weirdness and the sky-high mathematics required to precisely formulate and quantize string theory, I've come to appreciate how it illuminates potential pathways toward fully realizing Albert Einstein's dream of a unified description of reality where gravity blends seamlessly with quantum mechanics. It offers the tantalizing prospect of finally achieving a complete theory of everything. Of course, string theory remains very much a work in progress, with many deep questions yet to be resolved through future research and potential experiments. And it is just one of several competing proposals for how to construct a quantum theory of gravity. But the sheer creativity, boldness, and potential explanatory power of string theory captures my imagination like nothing else.

With this book, my goal is to share that sense of awe and excitement for string theory's potential with readers of all backgrounds. While inevitably I'll have to introduce some unavoidably complex concepts, I've done my best throughout to explain the core ideas and real-world implications of string theory in an accessible way, frequently drawing on analogies to more familiar examples wherever possible. My greatest hope is that after finishing this book, you'll come away appreciating why string theory is one of the most profound and ambitious undertakings in the history of human intellectual endeavor, even if some of its deepest mysteries remain unresolved for now. By synthesizing input from leading voices across physics and mathematics, I aim to provide a clear window into both the incredible progress already made as well as the towering challenges that still lie ahead.

I am also very grateful to my father Nagaraju Talari and my mother Rangaji Uma Bandi for the love and support they have provided me with. I am also grateful to my friends Aaron Sengupta, Prannoy Chowdury and Shivang Shrivastava for their assistance during the writing of this book. A very special thanks to my mentors Mr. Sriram Subramanian and Mr. Partha Chakraborty for guiding me while I journey through the vast world of theoretical physics which I'm still gaining knowledge on and have a lot more to accomplish.

\- Siddharth Talari

May 2024

1

INTRODUCTION

In the 1960s, the field of physics was experiencing a revolution with the rapid development of quantum mechanics. This new way of understanding science promised a radically different view of the universe, focusing on the behavior of atoms and subatomic particles. However, some physicists were not entirely satisfied with the idea that the smallest building blocks of matter were point-like particles, such as electrons and quarks. While quantum mechanics successfully described the microscopic world, combining it with Einstein's theory of general relativity (which describes gravity and the behavior of massive objects) led to puzzling problems and inconsistencies. Physicists realized that a new approach was needed to reconcile these two fundamental theories.

It was in this context that Dr. Leonard Susskind, working at Yeshiva University, had a bold idea: What if particles weren't really point-like at all, but instead were tiny strings vibrating in a higher-dimensional space? Around the same time, physicist Yoichiro Nambu was working on the strong nuclear force, which holds the nucleus of an atom together. He realized that treating the particles involved as tiny strings rather than point-like objects could explain the behavior of this force. Meanwhile, in the Netherlands, Gerard't Hooft was exploring similar ideas and realized that treating particles as strings could solve some of the problems plaguing existing theories.

At first, these ideas seemed strange and even a bit far-fetched. After all, how could something as tiny as a subatomic particle be a string? But as these physicists and others continued to explore and develop these ideas, they realized that string theory could potentially resolve many of the puzzles and inconsistencies that had been plaguing physics for decades. But first let's just address the elephant in the room here: What exactly is String Theory?

Imagine you have a piece of string. Now, imagine that this string is incredibly tiny, smaller than even the smallest particle you can think of. In fact, it's so small that it's impossible to see with our eyes or even the most powerful microscopes. This tiny string is vibrating, and its vibrations create everything we see in the universe – from the smallest particles to the largest stars and galaxies. String theory suggests that at the most fundamental level, the universe is made up of these tiny, vibrating strings. Just like different notes on a guitar string produce different sounds, the different vibrations of these strings give rise to all the different particles and forces that make up our universe. Now, let's think about something familiar: a jump rope. When you swing a jump rope, the rope takes on different shapes and patterns depending on how you swing it. In a similar way, the vibrations of these strings can create different shapes and patterns, which represent the various particles and forces we observe in nature.

For example, imagine that a particular vibration pattern of a string represents an electron, one of the fundamental particles that make up atoms. Another vibration pattern might represent a quark, which is a building block of protons and neutrons found in the nucleus of atoms. Different vibration patterns give rise to different particles, each with its own unique properties and behaviors. But why is string theory so important? Well, it offers a way to unify all the fundamental forces of nature – gravity, electromagnetism, and the strong and weak nuclear forces – into a single, coherent theory. This means that string theory could potentially explain the workings of the entire universe with a simple set of principles. Imagine trying to understand a complex machine without knowing how all its parts fit together. String theory is like having a blueprint that shows how all the different pieces of the universe are connected and work together in harmony.

Of course, string theory is still a work in progress, and there are many unanswered questions and challenges that scientists are working to solve. But the idea of tiny, vibrating strings as the fundamental building blocks of the universe is a fascinating concept that has captured the imagination of scientists and non-scientists alike.

In the chapters ahead, we'll dive deeper into the world of string theory, exploring its origins, its implications, and the mysteries that still surround this remarkable theory. Get ready to embark on an exciting journey into the tiniest realms of the universe and discover how these tiny strings could hold the key to understanding everything around us.

Fig. 1

2

DIMENSIONS

In our everyday lives, we experience three dimensions of space – length, width, and height – and one dimension of time. We can move forward, backward, left, right, up, and down. But what if there were more dimensions beyond the ones we can perceive directly?

String theory proposes the existence of extra dimensions, hidden from our senses, where these tiny, vibrating strings exist and dance their cosmic dance. This idea may seem strange and hard to imagine, but let's try to explore it with some analogies and thought experiments. Imagine you are playing the game "Super Mario Bros" from 1985. We all know that the game is two dimensional and you can only mostly move left and right. Now shift all the way to today, we barely have any mainstream two dimensional games anymore. We've evolved to a world of three dimensional, a more advanced, realistic gaming setup; where the gaming world is filled with shooters, racing games and fantasies. Now, it's general knowledge that a game console made in 1985, manufactured only for two dimensional games at the time, cannot perceive the three dimensional games.

Just like the game console can't fully comprehend the third dimension, we may be unable to directly perceive the extra dimensions proposed by string theory. These additional dimensions could be hiding in the nooks and crannies of reality, beyond our senses' ability to detect them. Another way to think about higher dimensions is through the analogy of a flat land and a land of hills. Imagine a two-dimensional world, where everything is flat and only has length and width. Now, imagine introducing a third dimension, height, into this world. Suddenly, you can have hills, valleys, and mountains – features that were impossible to conceive of in the flat, two-dimensional world. In a similar way, string theory suggests that by introducing extra dimensions beyond the three spatial dimensions and one time dimension we experience, new possibilities and features of the universe can emerge, like the hills and valleys in the three-dimensional world.

These extra dimensions could be incredibly small, curled up, or even existing in a different realm altogether, which is why we don't directly experience them in our daily lives. But their existence could help explain some of the deepest mysteries of the universe, such as the nature of gravity and the unification of all fundamental forces. The current version of string theory takes place in 10 dimensions, whereas an even more hypothetical über-string theory known as M-theory requires 11. We shall discuss this version of our topic in later chapters. While the concept of extra dimensions may seem mind-bending at first, it's important to remember that our senses and experiences are limited to the familiar dimensions we perceive. Just as the ant can't fully comprehend three dimensions, we may be limited in our ability to directly experience higher dimensions. But with the help of mathematics, physics, and our imagination, we can begin to explore and understand these unseen realms.

In the next chapter, we'll dive deeper into the fascinating world of string theory and explore how these extra dimensions and the vibrating strings within them could hold the key to understanding the origins of the universe and the fundamental forces that shape our reality.

Fig. 2 - Extra Dimensions in Space

3

DUALITY

Duality is the idea that two seemingly different physical situations or theories can actually be equivalent or related to each other in a profound way. It's like looking at the same object from two different angles and realizing that it's the same thing, just from a different perspective. First of all, we must understand that string theory is not just one interpretation but several different interpretations and has many versions based on one's research and understanding. But traditionally, there were only 5 widely accepted versions of string theory which are Type 1, Type IIA, Type IIB, SO(32) heterotic, and E8xE8 heterotic, until it all changed in 1995. There are two types of duality that are particularly important: S-duality and T-duality. Let's explore these concepts using some simple analogies and examples.

S-duality is like looking in a mirror. Imagine you're standing in front of a mirror, and you see your reflection. Your reflection looks just like you, but it's reversed – what's on your left is now on the right, and vice versa. In a similar way, S-duality suggests that there are different versions of string theory that are mirror images of each other, but they're fundamentally related and describe the same underlying reality. One version of string theory might involve strings that are open-ended, like a long piece of string with two loose ends. The other version might involve strings that are closed-loop, like a rubber band or a circular piece of string. At first, these two versions of string theory might seem unrelated and distinct, just like the person and the building on the two sides of the coin. However, S-duality tells us that these two versions are actually deeply connected and are two different perspectives of the same fundamental theory. It's like having two different languages that describe the same thing. One language might use words like "open string" and "endpoint," while the other language might use words like "closed string" and "loop." Although the words are different, they are ultimately describing the same concept – the tiny, vibrating strings that make up the universe.

T-duality, on the other hand, is like looking at a cylinder from different angles. Imagine you have a cylindrical tube, and you look at it from one end. It appears to be a circle. But if you look at it from the side, it seems like a long, rectangular shape. These two perspectives are different, but they're both describing the same object – the cylinder.One way to describe strings is by imagining them as tiny, vibrating strands that are open-ended, like a piece of string with two loose ends. In this description, we might focus on how the strings move and vibrate in a linear or open-ended fashion. The other way to describe strings is by imagining them as closed loops, like a rubber band or a circular piece of string. In this description, we might focus on how the strings wrap around and vibrate within circular or closed dimensions.

At first glance, these two descriptions might seem completely different, just like the circular and rectangular views of the cylindrical object. However, T-duality tells us that these two descriptions are actually equivalent and related to each other in a profound way. It's like having two different languages that describe the same object, but one language focuses on the circular aspect, while the other language focuses on the linear aspect. Although the words and descriptions are different, they are ultimately talking about the same thing – the cylindrical object or, in the case of string theory, the behavior of tiny, vibrating strings. So basically, all that T- Duality focuses on is uniting the different perspectives of same theory in different angles.

All in all, duality acts as a translation key, allowing physicists to move between the different versions of string theory and to see the underlying connections and relationships between them. It's like being bilingual and being able to switch between the two languages seamlessly, understanding that they are both describing the same reality, just from different perspectives. This duality helps physicists to simplify and unify their understanding of string theory, just like realizing that the person and the building on the two sides of the coin are actually part of the same object. It allows them to translate insights and discoveries from one version of the theory to the other, making it easier to explore and understand the deep principles that govern the behavior of strings and the universe they shape. So, while the different versions of string theory might seem different on the surface, duality reminds us that they are ultimately two sides of the same coin, two perspectives of the same fundamental reality, waiting to be fully understood and appreciated.

Fig. 3 - A string with a "closed loop"

21

4

BRANES

In our exploration of string theory, we've learned about the tiny, vibrating strings that could be the fundamental building blocks of the universe and how their intricate dance gives rise to the particles and forces we observe. We've also delved into the fascinating concepts of extra dimensions and dualities, which provide new perspectives on these strings and their behavior.

But there's another intriguing aspect of string theory that we haven't yet explored – the idea of branes.

Branes, short for "membranes," are higher-dimensional objects that exist within the realm of string theory. While strings are one-dimensional objects, branes can have two, three, or even more dimensions. This concept of things existing in higher dimensions might seem pretty overwhelming at first but let's just take a step back and try to simplify this. We, as three-dimensional beings, might have difficulty fully comprehending the higher-dimensional objects proposed by string theory. We can only perceive cross-sections or "shadows" of these objects in our three-dimensional world. But just like a two-dimensional creature can understand the concept of a three-dimensional object by observing its cross-sections, we can begin to grasp the idea of branes by studying their lower-dimensional manifestations.

So, what exactly are these branes? Well, let's start with the simplest example. Imagine a soap bubble floating in the air. The surface of the soap bubble is a two-dimensional membrane – it has length and width but no thickness (or very little thickness, at least). In string theory, these two-dimensional branes are thought to exist within the higher-dimensional space where strings reside. Now, let's take it a step further. Imagine a stack of soap bubbles, one on top of the other. Each bubble represents a two-dimensional membrane, but when you combine them, they create a three-dimensional object – a "three-brane." These three-branes are incredibly important in string theory because they are thought to represent the universe we live in. Our three-dimensional space could be a three-brane existing within a higher-dimensional space populated by strings and other branes.

But that's not all! String theory also proposes the existence of even higher-dimensional branes, such as four-branes, five-branes, and so on. These higher-dimensional branes are like vast, multi-dimensional landscapes or universes within the overall fabric of string theory. They could have mind-bending properties and behaviors that are difficult for us to comprehend from our three-dimensional perspective. For example, imagine a four-brane – an object with four spatial dimensions (length, width, height, and an additional dimension we can't directly perceive). From our three-dimensional viewpoint, we might only see cross-sections or "shadows" of this four-brane, much like the two-dimensional creature can only see cross-sections of a three-dimensional object.

The concept of branes opens up a whole new realm of possibilities within string theory. They provide a way to understand how our three-dimensional universe might be embedded within a higher-dimensional space and how it could be connected to other universes or higher-dimensional realms. Branes also play a crucial role in understanding the fundamental forces of nature, such as gravity and electromagnetism. Some theories suggest that these forces might be manifestations of how strings and branes interact and move within the higher-dimensional space. While the idea of branes might seem abstract and challenging to visualize, it's important to remember that our understanding of the universe has been continually expanded by exploring concepts that were once thought to be impossible or beyond our comprehension.

Just as we've come to understand the three-dimensional world we live in, despite our initial limitations as two-dimensional creatures, exploring the realm of branes and higher dimensions could unlock new insights into the fundamental nature of reality and the universe we call home.

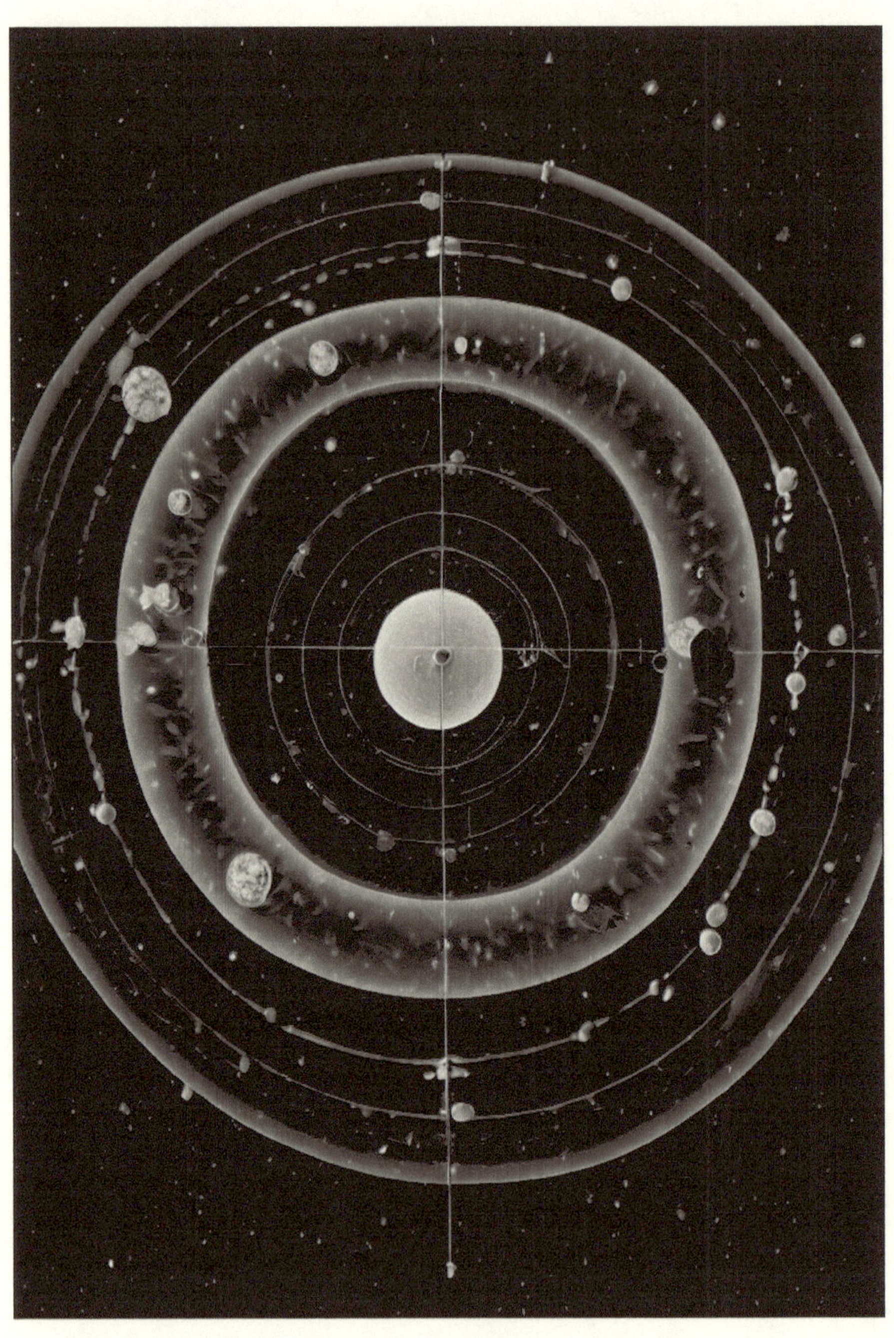

Fig. 4 - Branes in outer space (Abstract)

5

M-Theory

Now that we have the very basics of string theory out of the way, let's focus on the biggest question - How does string theory unite everything in the universe?

M-theory is often referred to as the "mother of all theories" or the "theory of everything" in the realm of string theory. It's a proposed unified theory that could potentially bring together all the different versions of string theory and explain the fundamental nature of the universe in a single, coherent framework. Now, you might be thinking, "Wait a minute, I thought string theory was already supposed to be the ultimate theory of everything?" Well, it turns out that string theory itself has multiple versions or "flavors," each with its own strengths and limitations as we have discussed in the previous chapters. It's like having different types of ice cream – vanilla, chocolate, strawberry, and so on. Each flavor has its own unique taste and characteristics, but they're all still ice cream at their core. Similarly, the different versions of string theory share common principles and ideas, but they have distinct mathematical formulations and approaches. M-theory aims to be the "ultimate ice cream sundae" that combines and unifies all these different flavors of string theory into one comprehensive theory.

But what exactly is M-theory, and how does it achieve this unification? Well, to be honest, even the world's leading physicists aren't entirely sure! M-theory is still a work in progress, and its complete mathematical formulation and details are yet to be fully understood. However, we do know some intriguing clues and hints about M-theory, and it's these tantalizing glimpses that have captured the imagination of scientists and sparked a relentless pursuit to unravel its mysteries. One of the key ideas behind M-theory is that it exists in a higher-dimensional space, with more dimensions than the ten or eleven dimensions proposed by the various versions of string theory. These extra dimensions could hold the key to unifying all the different string theories and explaining the fundamental nature of reality.

Imagine a vast, multidimensional landscape where all the different versions of string theory exist as different regions or "neighborhoods." M-theory is like a map or a blueprint that shows how all these regions are connected and how they fit together into a larger, coherent whole. Just like a city planner might have a comprehensive map of a metropolis, showing how all the different neighborhoods, roads, and landmarks are interconnected, M-theory aims to provide a unified view of the entire "string theory universe" and how its various components relate to one another. Another intriguing aspect of M-theory is its potential to incorporate and explain the concept of branes – those higher-dimensional objects we discussed in the previous chapter. Some theories suggest that M-theory could be a "theory of branes," where these multidimensional objects play a crucial role in shaping the fundamental fabric of reality.

Imagine a vast, multidimensional tapestry woven from strings and branes, with M-theory providing the intricate pattern and design that brings it all together. Just as a skilled weaver can create intricate designs by carefully arranging threads and patterns, M-theory could be the guiding principle that governs the interactions and movements of strings and branes in a higher-dimensional space. Of course, visualizing and understanding these higher-dimensional concepts is no easy task, even for the most seasoned physicists. But that's precisely what makes M-theory so exciting and challenging – it pushes the boundaries of our imagination and our understanding of the universe.

While the complete picture of M-theory remains elusive, the tantalizing glimpses and clues we've uncovered so far have sparked a relentless pursuit among scientists to unravel its mysteries. It's a quest that could potentially revolutionize our understanding of the fundamental nature of reality and unlock new realms of knowledge and discovery.

Fig. 5 - Imagination of M-Theory

6

Black Holes

Black holes are among the most enigmatic and captivating objects in the universe. They are regions of spacetime where the gravitational pull is so intense that nothing, not even light, can escape its grasp once it ventures too close. These cosmic behemoths have puzzled and intrigued scientists for decades, and their study has led to some of the most profound insights into the nature of gravity, quantum mechanics, and the very fabric of reality.

One of the most remarkable discoveries in the study of black holes came in the 1970s, when physicists Jacob Bekenstein and Stephen Hawking independently proposed a formula that relates the entropy of a black hole to its surface area and other properties. Entropy is a measure of disorder or randomness in a system, and it plays a crucial role in the laws of thermodynamics. Surprisingly, Bekenstein and Hawking showed that black holes possess entropy, which is directly proportional to the surface area of their event horizon – the boundary beyond which nothing can escape the black hole's gravitational pull.

The Bekenstein-Hawking formula states that the entropy of a black hole is given by:

Where:

- **S** is the entropy of the black hole

- **A** is the surface area of the event horizon

- **c** is the speed of light

- **G** is Newton's gravitational constant

- **ħ** (h-bar) is the Planck constant, a fundamental constant in quantum mechanics

This formula was a groundbreaking revelation because it suggested that black holes, which were once thought to be devoid of any thermodynamic properties, actually behave like thermodynamic objects with well-defined entropy. But why is this formula so important, and what does it have to do with string theory? Well, the Bekenstein-Hawking formula hints at a deep connection between gravity, quantum mechanics, and the nature of spacetime itself – a connection that string theory might be able to shed light on.

In the realm of string theory, black holes are not just massive objects with intense gravitational fields; they are also considered to be highly curved regions of spacetime, where the fabric of reality itself is stretched and warped to its limits. According to string theory, spacetime is not a smooth, continuous entity but rather a complex tapestry woven from vibrating strings and branes. In regions of extreme curvature, such as near black holes, this tapestry becomes highly distorted and tangled, leading to mind-bending phenomena that challenge our understanding of physics. One of the most intriguing aspects of black holes in string theory is the idea of "black hole entropy." Just like the Bekenstein-Hawking formula suggests, black holes are thought to possess a significant amount of entropy, which is related to the number of different microscopic configurations or "states" that the strings and branes can take on within the black hole's event horizon.

Imagine a vast, tangled web of strings and branes, all vibrating and interacting in countless different ways. Each of these configurations represents a different microscopic state of the black hole, and the total number of possible states determines the black hole's entropy. But why is this entropy important? Well, it turns out that the entropy of a black hole is intimately related to the information paradox – one of the deepest mysteries in theoretical physics.

The information paradox is a thought experiment proposed by physicist John Preskill in the 1990s, which highlighted a seeming contradiction between the principles of quantum mechanics and the behavior of black holes. According to quantum mechanics, information about the state of a system can never be truly lost or destroyed. Every bit of information should be preserved, even after the system undergoes a transformation or interaction. However, when an object falls into a black hole, it seems to disappear from our observable universe, taking all its information with it. This apparent loss of information violates the principles of quantum mechanics and creates a paradox that has puzzled physicists for decades.

String theory might hold the key to resolving this paradox by providing a deeper understanding of the nature of black holes and the microscopic structure of spacetime. According to string theory, the information about an object that falls into a black hole is not truly lost; it becomes encoded in the intricate patterns and configurations of the strings and branes within the black hole's event horizon. In other words, the information is stored in the black hole's entropy, which is related to the number of possible microscopic states of the strings and branes. This idea suggests that black holes are not truly "black" or devoid of information; they are intricate repositories of information encoded in the fabric of spacetime itself.

The study of black holes and their connection to string theory is an active area of research, with scientists and theorists constantly pushing the boundaries of our understanding. One of the most exciting prospects in this field is the possibility of directly observing the effects of quantum gravity and the microscopic structure of spacetime near the event horizon of black holes. While this is an immense challenge due to the extreme conditions and distances involved, future advancements in observational techniques and theoretical models might make it possible.

For example, the Event Horizon Telescope (EHT), a global array of radio telescopes, has already provided groundbreaking images of the supermassive black hole at the center of the M87 galaxy. As this technology continues to advance, it could potentially reveal clues about the behavior of spacetime and the imprints of string theory near the event horizon. Additionally, future particle accelerators and high-energy experiments might produce microscopic black holes or other exotic phenomena that could shed light on the quantum nature of gravity and the validity of string theory predictions. While the study of black holes and their connection to string theory may seem esoteric and detached from our everyday lives, it is important to recognize that many of the greatest scientific discoveries and technological advancements have emerged from the pursuit of fundamental knowledge and the exploration of the universe's deepest mysteries. The development of quantum mechanics and the understanding of the behavior of subatomic particles have led to a vast array of technologies, from transistors and computer chips to lasers and medical imaging devices. Similarly, the study of black holes and string theory could pave the way for new breakthroughs and innovations that we can't even imagine today.

Perhaps the understanding of quantum gravity and the microscopic structure of spacetime could lead to new forms of energy production, advanced materials with mind-bending properties, or even the development of technologies that could one day allow us to explore the depths of black holes and the fabric of reality itself. As we continue to unravel the mysteries of black holes and their connection to string theory, we embark on a journey that not only expands our understanding of the universe but also challenges our imagination and pushes the boundaries of human knowledge. It is a quest that has captivated scientists and thinkers for generations, and it promises to reveal even more profound insights into the nature of reality in the years to come.

Fig. 6 - Black Hole

7

PHENOMENOLOGY

Phenomenology in physics is about taking the mathematical models and theories and finding ways to test them with experiments and observations. It's like connecting the dots between the abstract world of theoretical physics and the tangible world we experience. In this chapter, we will be discussing multiple topics in theoretical physics and how they are connected to the advancements made in string theory.

One of the exciting aspects of string theory is its prediction of new particles. These particles might be discovered in high-energy experiments, like those conducted with particle accelerators.

1. Particle Accelerators

Particle accelerators are machines that speed up particles to very high energies and smash them together. By observing the results, scientists can discover new particles and learn more about the fundamental building blocks of the universe.

The Large Hadron Collider (LHC) is the world's largest and most powerful particle accelerator. It helped discover the Higgs boson, a particle that gives other particles mass. String theory suggests there could be many more particles waiting to be discovered.

2. Supersymmetry

Supersymmetry is a concept in string theory that proposes every particle has a superpartner. These superpartners are heavier particles that we haven't yet observed. If supersymmetry is true, it could solve many puzzles in physics, like the nature of dark matter.

3. Dark Matter

Dark matter is mysterious stuff that makes up about 27% of the universe. We can't see it, but we know it's there because of its gravitational effects. Supersymmetry might explain what dark matter is, as some of the superpartner particles predicted by string theory could be the particles that make up dark matter.

4. Inflation

Inflation is the idea that the universe expanded extremely rapidly just after the Big Bang. String theory provides a framework for understanding inflation and its effects on the universe.

5. Compactification

String theory suggests that there are six or seven additional dimensions that are "compactified," or curled up so small that we can't see them. These extra dimensions could explain some of the strange behaviors of particles and forces.

6. Gravitational Waves

Gravitational waves are ripples in spacetime caused by violent events, like colliding black holes. The detection of gravitational waves has opened a new way to test theories like string theory.

7. Cosmic Microwave Background

The cosmic microwave background (CMB) is the afterglow of the Big Bang. By studying tiny variations in the CMB, scientists can learn about the early universe and test predictions made by string theory.

8. High-Energy Physics Experiments

High-energy physics experiments, like those conducted at the LHC, are crucial for testing string theory. Scientists look for signs of new particles and forces predicted by the theory.

While string theory is a promising framework, it's not without challenges.

I. Theoretical Hurdles

One of the biggest challenges is that string theory requires complex mathematics and many assumptions. Scientists are working hard to refine these ideas and make testable predictions.

II. Experimental Limitations

Current technology limits our ability to test string theory directly. However, future advancements in particle accelerators and space telescopes could provide new ways to explore these ideas.

III. The Multiverse

String theory suggests that our universe might be just one of many in a vast multiverse. This idea is still highly speculative, but it could explain why our universe has the properties it does.

String theory phenomenology is a vibrant field that bridges the gap between theoretical predictions and experimental discoveries. While we have much to learn, the potential for new breakthroughs is enormous. Whether through discovering new particles, understanding dark matter, or uncovering the mysteries of the universe's origins, string theory holds the promise of a deeper understanding of the cosmos.

Fig. 7 - Gravitational Waves

8

CONNECTIONS TO MATHEMATICS

One of the most fascinating aspects of string theory is just how tightly it is connected to various branches of pure mathematics. Not only does string theory make use of many advanced mathematical concepts, but it has also motivated new mathematical discoveries and opened up entirely new fields of study.

The mathematical underpinnings of string theory go far beyond what students typically encounter in high school math classes. While algebra, geometry, and calculus provide an essential foundation, string theorists must dive into more esoteric realms like topology, algebraic geometry, representation theory, and even number theory and combinatorics. At first glance, the connections between particle physics and these abstract mathematical disciplines might seem puzzling. How could the behavior of subatomic strings and the fabric of spacetime possibly be related to mathematical abstractions like the classification of high-dimensional shapes? As we'll explore in this chapter, not only are these mathematics/physics links real, but they provide powerful insights into both mathematics and physics. Indeed, many cutting-edge mathematicians are now motivated by questions stemming from theoretical physics, and physicists increasingly rely on mathematical techniques that were initially developed with no applications in mind.

Mirror Symmetry

Imagine you have two very different-looking shapes - one is a bumpy sphere with lots of dents, and the other is a cube with tunnels drilled through it. They look completely unalike, right? Well, in string theory, scientists discovered that sometimes two shapes that appear totally different can actually be mirrors of each other! This means that even though the sphere and cube look really different on the outside, they are sort of like reversed versions of the same underlying thing. It's kind of like those weird mirror images you see in funhouses or carnival rides. If you look in one mirror, you see yourself as a skinny stretched out noodle person. But then if you turn a corner and look in another mirror, you appear as a short, wide gummy bear! The mirrors are showing you very different-looking reflections, but it's still just you on the inside.

The bizarre thing about mirror symmetry is that not only do the two shapes look different visually, but their geometries and mathematical descriptions are completely swapped around too. It would be like taking the equation for a sphere and mapping it to the equation for a cube. Even though scientists expected completely different shapes to give different results when studying them, the mirror shapes actually give the exact same results for all the physics calculations! It's as if the funhouse mirrors are showing you two bodies that look totally different on the outside, but have the same heart, lungs, and organs on the inside.

No one fully understands why mirror symmetry works and why these mirror image shapes are connected so deeply. But scientists have figured out some of the math rules that relate one mirror shape to its partner. And mirror symmetry has allowed them to solve physics problems that were originally super hard by mapping them to an equivalent mirror version that's much simpler.

So in string theory, just because two shapes look amazingly different doesn't mean they can't be mirrors of each other describing the same core physics! It's one of the strangest and most surprising discoveries in modern science.

Calabi-Yau Landscape and Topological String Theory

You know how in video games, there are different levels or worlds that the characters explore? Each world has its own unique landscape with mountains, rivers, cities etc. In string theory, which tries to understand everything in the universe, there are also different "worlds" or shapes that the universe can take. These special shapes are called Calabi-Yau spaces. Just like video game worlds, the Calabi-Yau spaces determine what kinds of things exist in that universe - the particles, forces etc. So physicists need to study and understand all the possible Calabi-Yau spaces to know what our universe and others could be like.

Now Calabi-Yau spaces are very complex shapes with lots of holes, handles and higher dimensions that are impossible to visualize. But smart physicists realized you don't actually need to know all the detailed curves and bumps. You just need to know some key features about the shape, like how many holes it has. It's like describing a video game world just by its number of cities, mountains, rivers etc. This is where topological string theory comes in. It focuses just on these keyhole/handle properties rather than the full geometry. Amazingly, by studying the shapes this simplified way, physicists can calculate really important properties of the universe that shape describes.

It's like if you could figure out what characters, powers, and levels exist in a video game, just by counting how many cities, mountains etc are in each world! That would be much easier than modeling every single rock and tree. So topological string theory is all about using math shortcuts based on counting holes/connections to understand the physics of different Calabi-Yau universes. It's letting physicists explore the entire "landscape" of possible string theory universes much more easily. Pretty clever, right?

Matrix Models, Lattice Methods and Computational Mathematics

String theory is all about these tiny vibrating strings that make up everything. But calculating what the strings are doing gets extremely complicated, like the hardest math you can imagine! It's kind of like having to solve a million algebra problems all combined together. So physicists had to come up with some clever tricks to simplify the calculations and make them possible to actually work through. Two of these tricks are called matrix models and lattice methods. Matrix models take the string theory equations and rewrite them using special grids called matrices. By reorganizing the math this way, it becomes easier to calculate on computers.

Lattice methods are another simplification. Instead of trying to work with the whole universe of strings at once, physicists put the strings on a grid or lattice that divides everything up into smaller, more manageable pieces. Then they can solve one box of the lattice at a time. It's kind of like instead of solving a huge connect-the-dots picture with 10,000 dots, you break it up into a bunch of tiny 10x10 grids that you can complete one-by-one. Using tricks like these along with extremely fast computers, physicists have been able to calculate some basic properties of strings that help us understand more about how the universe works. Of course, even with all these simplifications, the full mathematics of string theory is still hugely complex. So physicists have to be like super math geniuses who are also wizards with computers to make any progress at all! It's a good thing they have powerful tricks like matrix models and lattices in their toolkit.

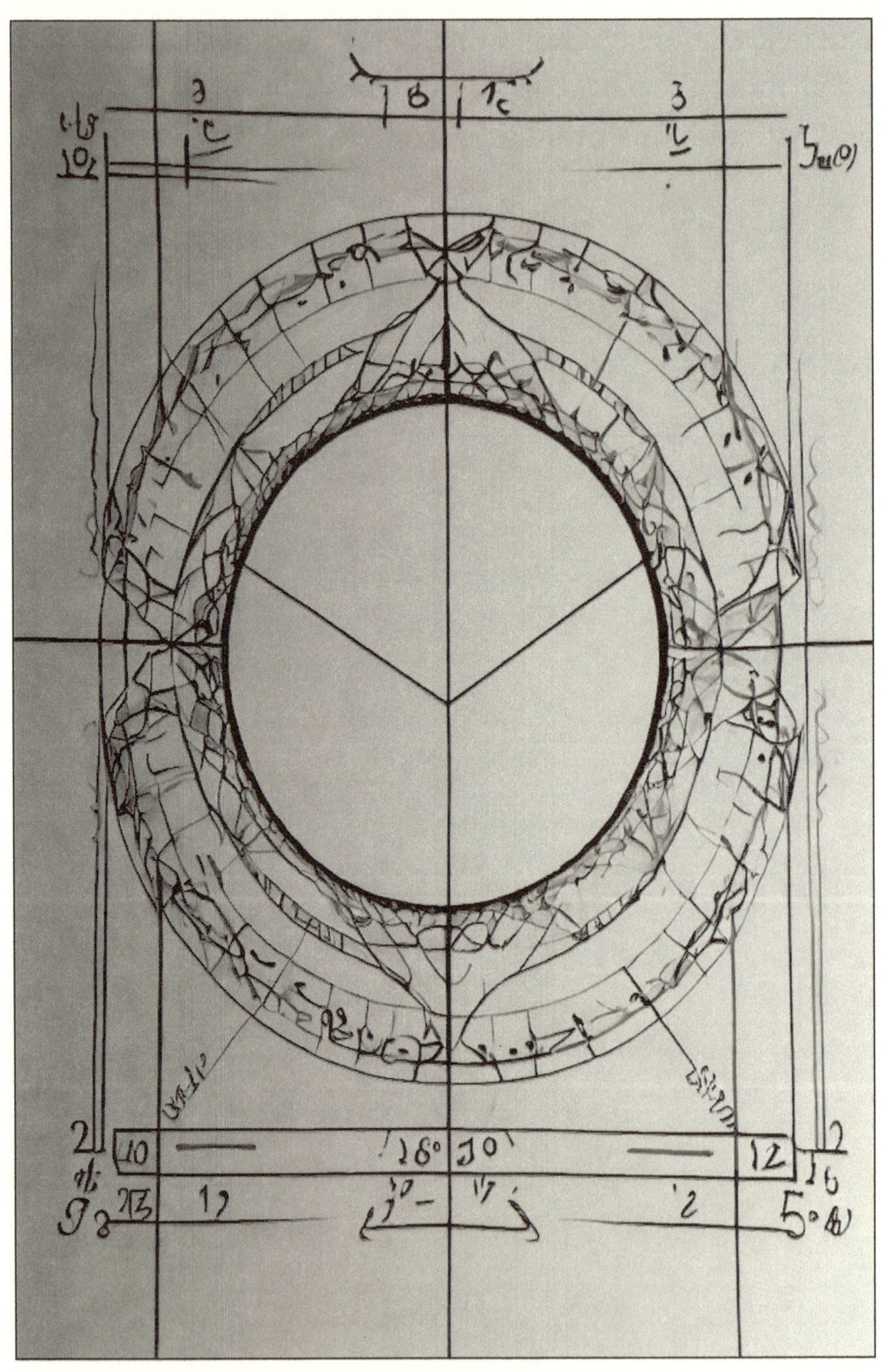

Fig. 8 - Mirror Theory in Mathematics

9
APPLICATIONS

String theory is a very complex subject that tries to understand everything in the entire universe. But even though it deals with some weird and mind boggling ideas, string theory has actually helped scientists understand some important things happening in the real world around us.

In this chapter, we'll talk about how string theory has helped physicists learn more about two big areas - the super-strong nuclear force that holds atomic nuclei together, and the largest things in the universe like galaxies, stars, and even the entire cosmos itself. String theory has provided new tools and insights that have advanced our knowledge in both these fields.

String Theory to Understand the Nuclear Force:

You've probably learned that atoms are made up of protons, neutrons and electrons. The protons and neutrons, which make up the nucleus or core of the atom, are held together extremely tightly by the nuclear strong force. This force is aptly named - it's one of the strongest forces in all of nature! The fundamental rules that describe this strong nuclear force are known, and are explained by a theory called quantum chromodynamics or QCD. But here's the tricky part - while we know the basic rules for QCD, actually calculating and predicting what happens when you combine a bunch of protons and neutrons is incredibly difficult with the regular mathematics we use. It's kind of like knowing all the rules of a very complex video game, but then not being able to predict what will happen when you try and play through the whole game from start to finish. There are too many steps and interactions to calculate.

This is where string theory has come to the rescue! Even though we can't use string theory directly to calculate the strong force, ideas and techniques borrowed from string theory have allowed physicists to develop new approximate methods and computer calculations to model the strong nuclear force. One key insight from string theory is that the strong force, which seems impossibly strong at low energies, may actually become a very feeble and simple force at much higher energies. By looking at "string theory-like" versions of QCD, physicists have been able to make predictions and see patterns that match experiments. Another powerful technique is to use string theory methods to study simplified "string-inspired" models that share some key properties with real-world QCD, like confinement. Even though not the entire real thing, studying these simplified String Land models has generated insights into why the strong force behaves so uniquely compared to other forces.

By giving physicists new mathematical techniques and perspectives, string theory has let them make progress calculating properties of protons, neutrons, and atomic nuclei in ways that were completely stuck before. Scientists can now run computer simulations, use approximation methods, and analyze string-inspired models to indirectly study the Strong Force. It's like being able to cheat at that impossibly difficult video game by finding glitches and exploits that let you bypass some of the most complex levels! String theory may not directly solve QCD, but it has provided a path through the maze.

Applications in Cosmology:

While the fundamental strings of string theory are unimaginably tiny - trillions upon trillions of times smaller than even the smallest subatomic particles - some physicists think that string theory may have left behind imprints and "fossils" that we could potentially observe in the largest things in the entire universe! You see, string theory doesn't just describe particles and forces in the present universe we live in today. Theories like cosmic string theory actually make predictions about how the universe itself could have begun from an unimaginably hot, dense, and rapidly expanding state known as the Big Bang.

In these earliest moments just after the Big Bang happened, the universe may have been governed by string theory physics rather than the gravity, particle physics, and other laws we see today. During this "string theory phase", the universe could have produced exotic objects and phenomena quite unlike anything we currently observe around us.

For example, some string theory models predict that during the extremely hot equilibrium state right after the Big Bang, higher dimensions may have been accessible and the universe could have produced massive string-like objects called cosmic strings. These cosmic strings would be truly enormous - perhaps light years or more across! Just like microscopic strings in string theory can vibrate and take different shapes, these gargantuan cosmic strings could also wobble around, intersect, and form wildly criss-crossing knots and loops. As the universe rapidly expanded and cooled, these knots and loops could have become frozen in place across the cosmos.

If cosmic strings exist, they would be mind-bogglingly heavy and dense, containing huge amounts of mass and gravitational force concentrated in a very thin string-like line. This could cause cosmic strings to act like lenses, bending and distorting light and images of galaxies behind them in peculiar ways. Astronomers have searched for signs of these cosmic string lenses and distortions, but so far the cosmic skies appear to be relatively smooth and string-free. However, the search continues as new telescopes and technology emerges.

Another prediction of string theory related to the Big Bang is the possible formation of various higher-dimensional defects, branes, and other topological anomalies in the fabric of the newborn universe. These defects could have included things like:

- **Monopoles** - Particles with just a single pole of a particular force field, rather than having two poles like most particles.

- **Domain walls** - Invisible planar sheets separating regions with different properties

- **Cosmic texture** - Knots and twists in condensates of new types of matter fields

Many of these exotic defects, if they existed, could have acted like tiny seeds around which ordinary matter began clumping together through gravitational attraction as the universe expanded. This could have led to areas with slightly higher or lower densities scattered across the sky. The cosmic microwave background (CMB) radiation, which is electromagnetic radiation left over from about 380,000 years after the Big Bang, provides a way to look for these telltale density fluctuations. If string theory defects provided the initial density seeds, we should be able to see slight temperature variations in the CMB corresponding to those seeds.

While astronomers have detected small temperature variations in the CMB corresponding to the slightly denser regions that eventually formed galaxies and galaxy clusters, so far there is no clear evidence of the specific patterns predicted by cosmic strings or other string defects. But the search continues!

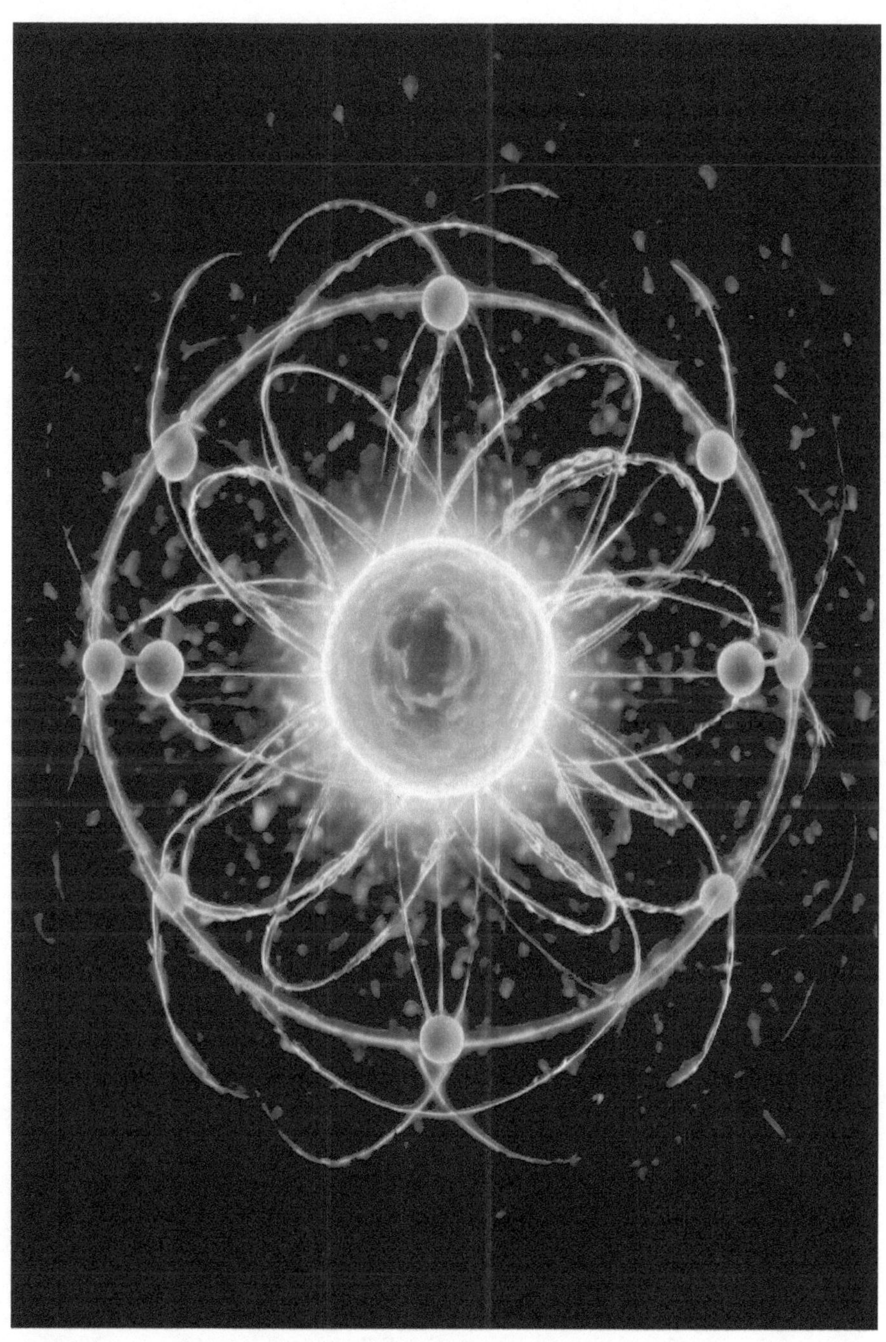

Fig. 9 - Nuclear Force

10

CONCLUSION AND CRITICISMS

Throughout this book, we've explored the incredible potential of string theory to revolutionize our understanding of the universe. Its novel ideas about tiny vibrating strings making up all matter and forces, higher dimensions beyond the familiar three of space, and even the possibility of parallel universes existing side-by-side have fired the imaginations of physicists and science enthusiasts alike. However, despite the amazing progress string theorists have made over the past few decades, many deep unanswered questions about the theory remain. String theory has also faced significant criticism from skeptics who argue it has failed to live up to its promise as a comprehensive "theory of everything" that Einstein spent his final years pursuing.

So in this final chapter, it's only fair that we take an honest look at the challenges, shortcomings, and criticisms still confronting string theory today. While the future remains bright, there are some daunting hurdles and alternative ideas that string theorists have yet to fully overcome or explain. It's important to understand these open problems before we can claim total success.

I. The Puzzle of Extra Dimensions

One of the most mind-bending aspects of string theory is the idea that as well as the three dimensions of space we experience in everyday life, there may be as many as seven extra dimensions of space out there that we somehow can't perceive directly. This higher-dimensional reality is a core prediction of string theory. But from our current vantage point, a universe with more than three spatial dimensions seems bizarre and hard to comprehend. How can these extra dimensions be out there in some form and we've never detected them? Where are they hiding?

String theorists have developed some creative explanations and scenarios to account for the invisibility of extra dimensions. One prominent idea speculates that while the three dimensions we see extend out indefinitely in size, the extra dimensions are somehow compactified, folded up or wrapped around themselves on unimaginably tiny scales, forming circular patterns or complex higher-dimensional shapes often visualized as multi-dimensional donuts or intricate knots. The patterns in which the extra dimensions may twist and wrap definitely affects the physics we can observe. So one reason we might not detect extra dimensions is if the compactification shape is extremely convoluted and complex on the smallest scales. But we still lack definitive experimental evidence for or against extra dimensions existing.

Even more fundamentally, string theorists have yet to conclusively show mathematically that string theory requires or truly predicts extra dimensions, rather than simply allowing them as a possibility. There are alternative proposals for reformulating string theory entirely in quantum lower dimensions. So the necessity of extra dimensions remains an unresolved issue from first principles. For a theory aiming to be as fundamental as possible, the idea of extra invisible dimensions that we are forced to just hypothesize about is understandably unsatisfying to many physicists. It would be far preferable if the reasons for extra dimensions naturally emerged from the basic equations and axioms of the theory alone.

II.   The Multiverse and Underdetermination Issues

Leading on from the uncertainties around extra dimensions is the controversial issue of the multiverse and the "landscape" of possible universes or vacuum solutions allowed within string theory. Based on our current formulation of string theory, it appears that depending on how the extra dimensions are wrapped and compactified, there could be an essentially infinite number of possible resulting vacuum universes or "bubble universes" allowed by the theory's equations, each with distinct properties like different particle types, forces and constants of nature. Our familiar universe, with its particular collection of particles, forces and constants we observe, would then be just one random possibility allowed within string theory's vast "landscape." This multiverse scenario is philosophically disturbing for many physicists. It potentially means that rather than string theory making strict, definite predictions about how our universe must be, it predicts virtually anything is possible across an infinite multiverse.

Critics argue this presents an acute problem of underdetermination - where the underlying theory fails to uniquely specify a solution for our actual observed universe. Instead of deriving our reality from first principles, string theorists must reverse engineer a vacuum solution that matches our universe in an ad hoc way. But there's no longer a single explanation for why things are the way they are.

String theory was meant to provide a comprehensive, unique "theory of everything" that would explain all the particles, forces and parameters of our universe based solely on fundamental principles. But the prospect of a vast multiverse landscape containing infinitely many possible universes seems to undermine that core goal. If we inhabit just one random universe out of an infinite multitude, all with different properties allowed by string theory, then how can string theory truly explain or predict the specific features of our universe? Those properties would be simply environmental accidents within the grander multiverse rather than following inevitably from the core theory itself. This underdetermination problem seems to rob string theory of its tremendous explanatory power as a theory of everything. If virtually any universe is possible, the theory fails to be uniquely predictive or to provide deeper reasons for why our universe has the particles, forces and constants it does.

Some string theorists have argued that we simply need to accept the multiverse as a possibility and find other statistical or anthropic reasons for our specific universe's properties. But many critics find this deeply unsatisfying from a scientific standpoint. They want a single, unique theoretical framework that can derive our universe from first principles rather than an "anything goes" multiverse.

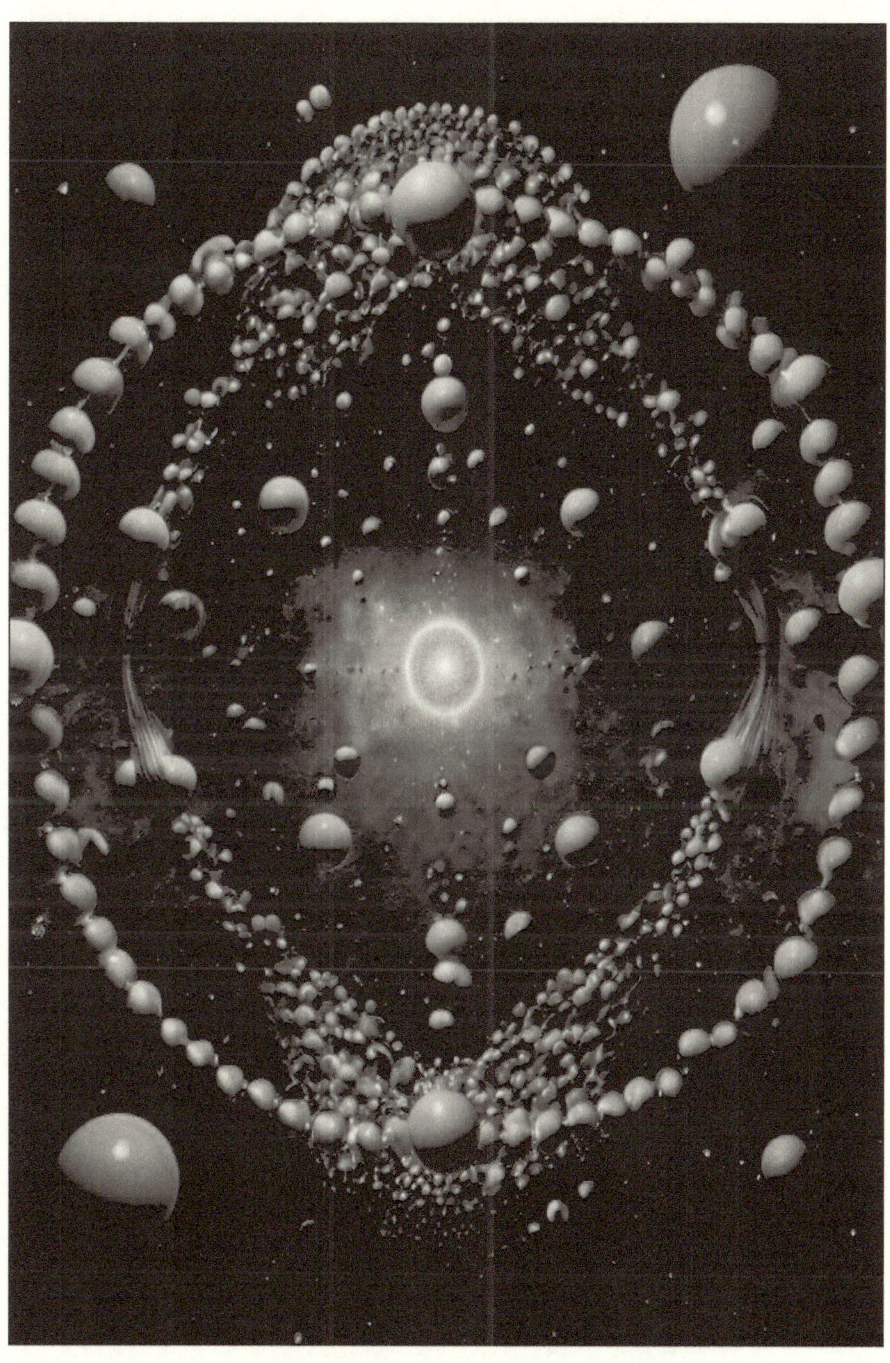

Fig. 10 - The Multiverse

GLOSSARY

AdS/CFT Correspondence - A conjectured relationship in string theory between certain string theories defined on anti-de Sitter spaces (AdS) and quantum field theories defined on the boundary of that space (CFT). Provides insights linking gravity and quantum field theories.

Anthropic Principle - The idea that observations we make about the universe may be constrained or selected by the requirements for life to exist. Used in some cosmic evolution models to potentially explain universal constants.

Big Bang - The cosmological model describing the universe as initially emerging from an extremely hot, dense singular state and rapidly expanding and cooling over billions of years to its present state.

Brane - A general term referring to any physical object that ties strings together or that strings can end on within string theory, including higher-dimensional membranes or D-branes.

Calabi-Yau Manifold - A specific category of 6-dimensional compact manifolds with special curvature properties that play a key role in string theory's extra dimensions and compactification schemes.

Compactification - The theoretical process in string theory and other higher-dimensional frameworks for constraining or wrapping up extra spatial dimensions to obtain 4-dimensional physics at low energies.

Cosmic Strings - Hypothetical massive, line-like imperfections predicted to form from high energies events like the Big Bang in certain cosmic string theory models of the early universe.

D-brane - Short for Dirichlet branes, these are non-perturbative objects in string theory that strings can begin or end on, providing an important mechanism for describing certain solitonic objects.

Gauge Theory - A type of quantum field theory based on fundamental forces described by connections in fiber bundles. Examples include electromagnetism described by a $U(1)$ gauge theory.

Gluon - The gauge particle that mediates the strong nuclear force between quarks in quantum chromodynamics (QCD), analogous to the photon for electromagnetism.

Hadron - A subatomic particle composed of quarks bound together by the strong nuclear force, including baryons like protons and neutrons, and mesons.

Heterotic String Theory - One of the five consistent superstring theories in 10 dimensions considered perturbatively finite. Combines both open and closed strings in a supersymmetric framework.

Kaluza-Klein Theory - An early 20th century model proposing that by adding an extra dimension to general relativity, one could geometrically unify gravity with gauge theories of electromagnetism.

M-Theory - A conjectured 11-dimensional theory whose low-energy limit recovers the various 10-dimensional superstring theories as different approximations or limits. Thought to unify all string theories.

Quantum Chromodynamics (QCD) - The fundamental quantum gauge field theory describing the strong nuclear force and interactions between quarks and gluons. Based on an $SU(3)$ gauge symmetry.

String Duality - Relationships between different string theories in various dimensions and limits that imply the theories are actually fully equivalent descriptions of the same underlying physics.

String Landscape - The potentially vast set of possible vacuum states or solutions allowed mathematically within string theory models with different values for constants, particles, etc.

T-Duality - A relationship in string theory where compact dimensions of one geometric space can be interchanged with the winding modes of strings in a dual geometry while preserving physics.

Type I String Theory - One of the five perturbatively consistent superstring theories in 10D involving both open and closed strings, related to the SO(32) gauge theory.

Type II String Theories - Two consistent superstring theories (IIA and IIB) formulated in 10 dimensions with differing supersymmetries and field contents. Central to M-theory and AdS/CFT.

Quantum Gravity - The longstanding challenge of formulating a complete, consistent quantum theory incorporating Einstein's general relativity able to describe gravitational fields on quantum scales.

www.ingramcontent.com/pod-product-compliance
Lightning Source LLC
Chambersburg PA
CBHW022109150726

47990CB00003B/1286